A Little
Fish Book
about

JOHN
THE
BAPTIST

Illustrated by Gordon Stowell

Zechariah and his wife Elizabeth loved God. But they were sad because they had no children and they were getting old.

Zechariah was a priest in the
Temple of Jerusalem. One day
when he was by himself in the
Temple, something wonderful
happened.

He saw the Angel Gabriel. Zechariah was afraid. "Don't be afraid," Gabriel said, "I have good news. Elizabeth is going to have a baby son. Name him John."

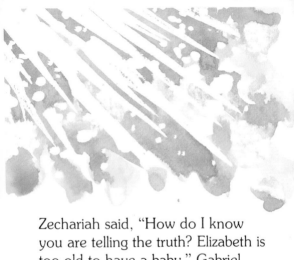

Zechariah said, "How do I know you are telling the truth? Elizabeth is too old to have a baby." Gabriel said, "Because you do not believe me, you will not be able to speak a word until after your baby is born."

When the baby was born, Elizabeth and Zechariah and all their friends were very happy. "His name is John," said Elizabeth.

"Why is his name John?" asked their friends. "No one in your family has that name."

"What shall we call him?" they asked Zechariah. Zechariah wrote, "His name is John."

As soon as Zechariah wrote this, he could speak again, just as the angel had promised.

John grew up. He went to live by himself in some wild lonely hills.

Crowds of people came to listen to him. He said, "Get ready. Soon God is sending us a Saviour."

When men and women and children were sorry for the wrong things they had done, John baptized them in the Jordan River.

News about John spread all over the country. One day Jesus came to John and said, "Baptize me, too."

So John and Jesus went into the
water. God spoke to Jesus.
He said, "You are my dear Son.
I am very pleased with you."

John was very glad! He knew Jesus was God's own Son. John told everyone about Jesus.

You can find the story of John the Baptist in the New Testament. It is in the book of Luke, chapter 1, verses 5 to 25, and also in Matthew, chapter 3, verses 1 to 17.

Little Fish Books about Bible People
ABRAHAM

Little Fish Books about Bible People
RUTH

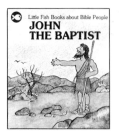

Little Fish Books about Bible People
JOHN THE BAPTIST

Little Fish Books about Bible People
PETER

 Little Fish Books